2012

	DATE DUE		
Cu aug 13			

WITHDRAWN

AUG -- 2013

Animals
on the Farm
Cows

Linda Aspen-Baxter
and Heather Kissock

www.av2books.com

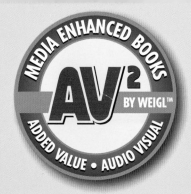

MEDIA ENHANCED BOOKS
AV²
BY WEIGL™
ADDED VALUE • AUDIO VISUAL

Go to **www.av2books.com**, and enter this book's unique code.

BOOK CODE

H854282

AV² by Weigl brings you media enhanced books that support active learning.

AV² provides enriched content that supplements and complements this book. Weigl's AV² books strive to create inspired learning and engage young minds in a total learning experience.

Your AV² Media Enhanced books come alive with...

Audio
Listen to sections of the book read aloud.

Video
Watch informative video clips.

Embedded Weblinks
Gain additional information for research.

Try This!
Complete activities and hands-on experiments.

Key Words
Study vocabulary, and complete a matching word activity.

Quizzes
Test your knowledge.

Slide Show
View images and captions, and prepare a presentation.

... and much, much more!

Published by AV² by Weigl
350 5th Avenue, 59th Floor New York, NY 10118
Website: www.av2books.com   www.weigl.com

Library of Congress Cataloging-in-Publication Data

Kissock, Heather.
 Cows / Heather Kissock and Linda Aspen-Baxter.
    p. cm. -- (Animals on the farm)
 ISBN 978-1-61690-925-3 (hardcover : alk. paper) -- ISBN 978-1-61690-571-2 (online)
 1. Dairy cattle--Juvenile literature. 2. Cows--Juvenile literature. I. Aspen-Baxter, Linda. II. Title.
 SF208.K57 2012
 636.2--dc23
                              2011023422

Printed in the United States of America in North Mankato, Minnesota
1 2 3 4 5 6 7 8 9 0 15 14 13 12 11

062011
WEP030611

Senior Editor: Heather Kissock   Art Director: Terry Paulhus

Weigl acknowledges Getty Images as the primary image supplier for this title.

Animals on the Farm

Cows

CONTENTS

I am a large farm animal. Farmers keep me for my meat and milk.

4

5

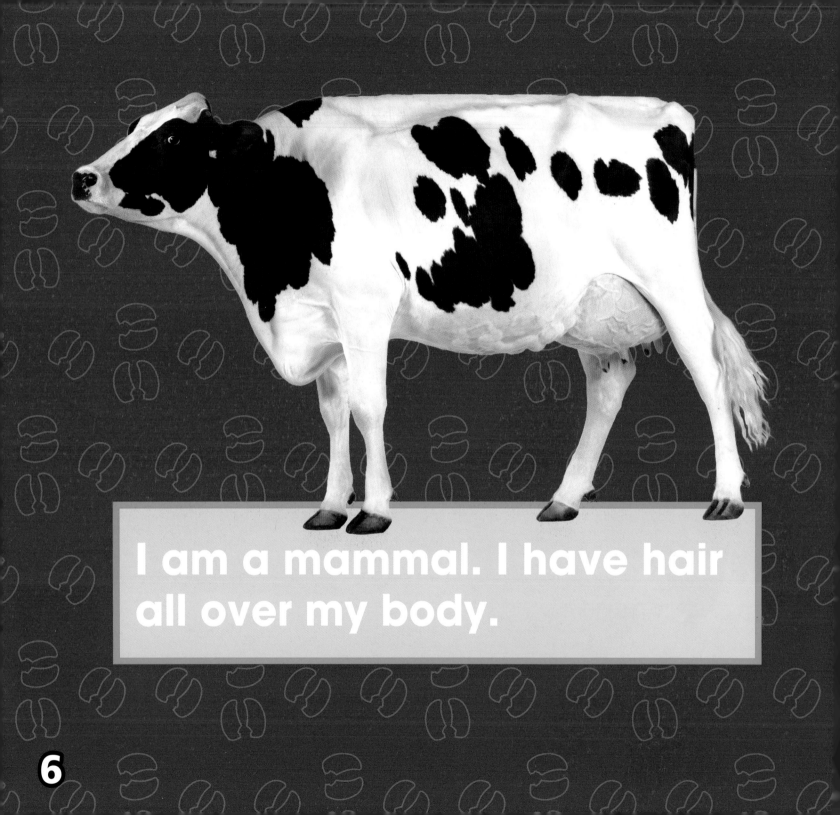

I am a mammal. I have hair all over my body.

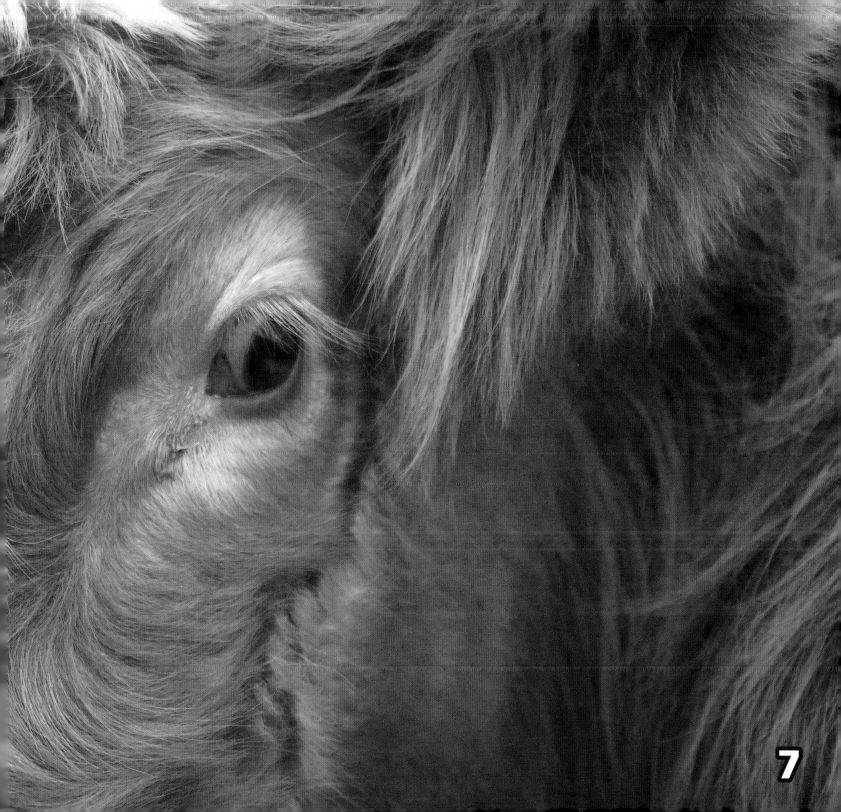

7

I use my four strong legs to walk and run. Each leg has a hoof at the end.

I have a long tail. I use it to swat insects off me.

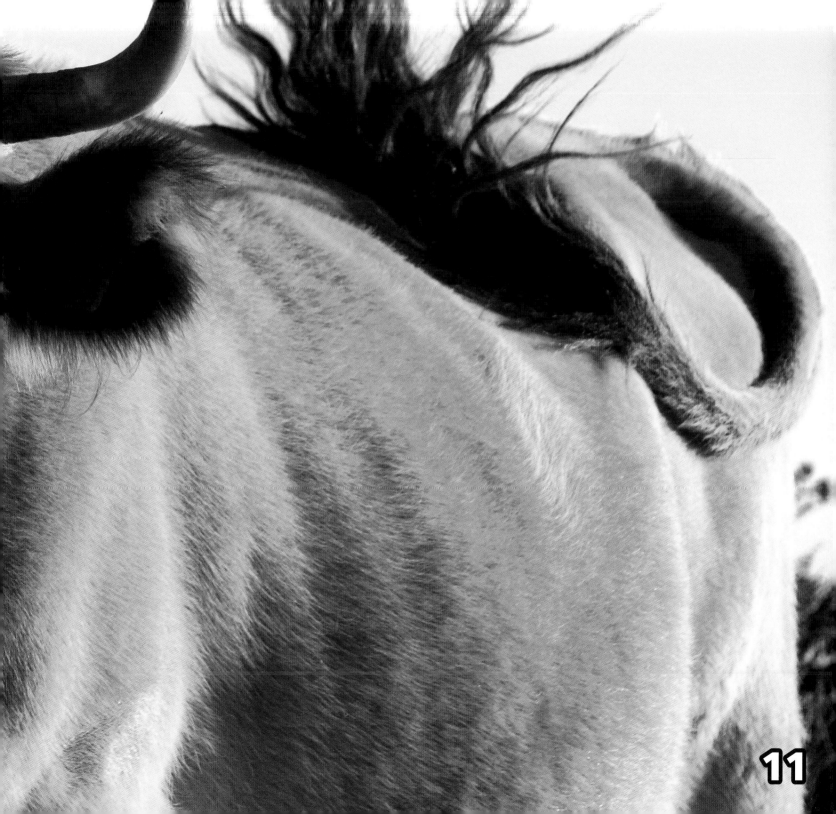

11

I eat grass, hay, and grains. I pull my food toward me with my tongue and bottom teeth.

13

14

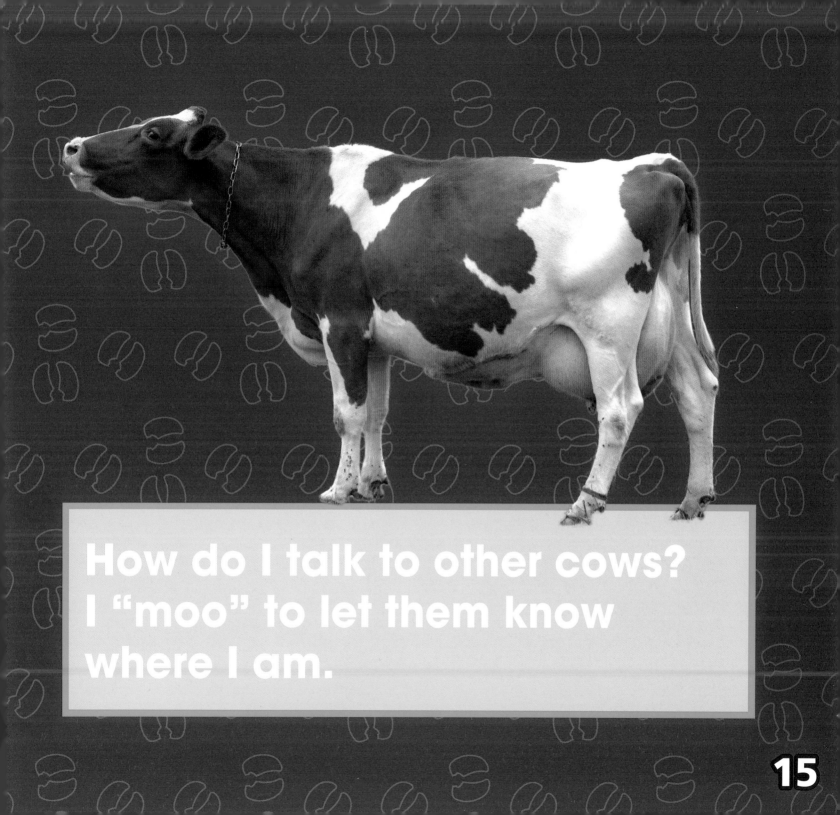

How do I talk to other cows? I "moo" to let them know where I am.

I like to be with other cows.
I lick my friends to show
I like them.

17

I sometimes have a baby in the spring.

18

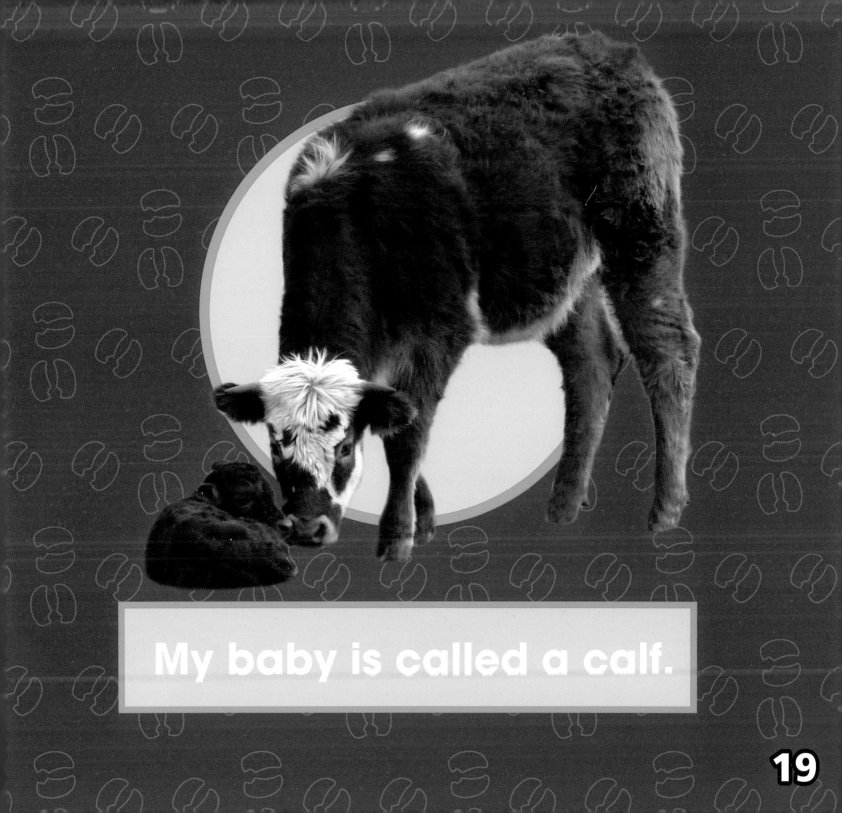

My baby is called a calf.

My calf stands shortly after it is born. Sometimes, it needs help getting up.

20

COW FACTS

This page provides more detail about the interesting facts found in the book. Simply look at the corresponding page number to match the fact.

Pages 4–5

Farmers keep cows for meat and milk. There are three main groups of cattle. They are grouped by their use or purpose. The three groups are beef cattle, dairy cattle, and dual-purpose cattle. Beef cattle are raised for their meat, while dairy cattle are raised for their milk. Dual-purpose cattle are used for both meat and milk.

Pages 6–7

Cows are mammals. Mammals have three main characteristics. All mammals grow hair or fur on their bodies. Mammals are also warm-blooded. This means they can produce their own body heat. As well, the female of any mammal species is able to make milk for its young to feed on.

Pages 8–9

Cows use their four strong legs to walk and run. At the bottom of each leg is a hoof. A cow is cloven-hoofed. This means that its feet are divided into two parts, like toes. When a cow is walking through mud, its toes spread out. This supports the cow in the mud and keeps it from sinking very far.

Pages 10–11

Cows have long tails. Their tails are most often used as a fly swatter, to rid themselves of insects that want to bite them. However, cows also use their tails to communicate. When their tails are hanging straight down, they are calm and relaxed. If they hold their tail between their legs, they are not feeling well.

Pages 12–13

Cows eat grass, hay, and grain. They have no top, front teeth. They pull their food toward them with their tongue and bottom teeth. Cows are ruminants. This means that their stomach has four parts to help break down food. Cows swallow their food and then spit it back up to chew it. This is called chewing cud.

Pages 14–15

Cows "moo" to let others know where they are. They also moo when they are looking for a mate, feeling uncomfortable, or in a playful mood. Babies will moo for their mother. If a mother cannot find her baby, however, she will bellow for it. This is a loud call.

Pages 16–17

Cows like to be with other cows. They are very social animals. This is because they are herd animals and are used to being in a group. Most cows will naturally follow the smartest and strongest members of the herd. Cows form friendships with other cows. They show affection by grooming and licking one another.

Pages 18–19

Cows have their babies in the spring. Babies are called calves. Cows carry their babies for about nine months before giving birth. After giving birth, a cow and her calf stay close together and form a strong bond. The calf is considered to be full grown when it is about 4 years of age.

Pages 20–21

Calves can stand shortly after they are born. Their legs are wobbly at first, but they quickly gain the strength needed to walk and run. A calf will weigh about 80 to 100 pounds (36 to 45 kilograms) at birth. By the time calves reach adulthood, they weigh anywhere from 800 to 2,500 pounds (362 to 1,134 kilograms).

WORD LIST

Research has shown that as much as 65 percent of all written material published in English is made up of 300 words. These 300 words cannot be taught using pictures or learned by sounding them out. They must be recognized by sight. This book contains 47 common sight words to help young readers improve their reading fluency and comprehension. This book also teaches young readers several important content words. These words are paired with pictures to aid in learning and improve understanding.

Page	Sight Words First Appearance	Page	Content Words First Appearance
4	I, a, large, animal, keep, me, for, my, and	4	farmers, meat, milk
6	have, all, over	6	body, hair, mammal
8	use, four, to, walk, run, each, has, at, the, end	8	hoof, legs
10	long, it, off	10	insects, tail
13	eat, food, with	13	grains, grass, hair, teeth, tongue
15	how, do, talk, other, let, them, where	15	cows
17	like, be, show	17	friends
18	sometimes, in	18	baby, spring
19	is, called	19	calf
20	after, needs, help, getting, up		

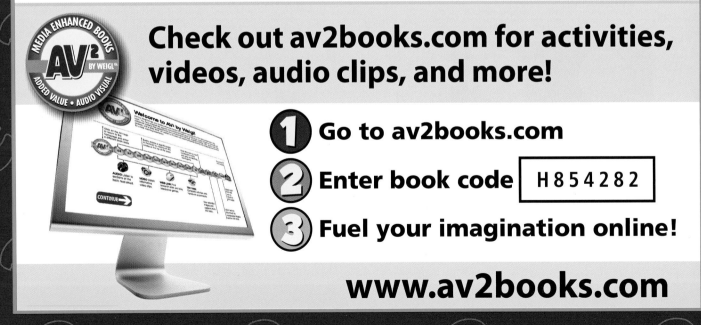

Check out av2books.com for activities, videos, audio clips, and more!

Welcome to AV² by Weigl!

AUDIO VIDEO WEB LINK

CONTINUE ➡

1 Go to av2books.com

2 Enter book code H 8 5 4 2 8 2

3 Fuel your imagination online!

www.av2books.com